THE BABY FLIGHT
a true story

Paul H. Karrer

PARK PLACE PUBLICATIONS
PACIFIC GROVE, CALIFORNIA

$\mathcal{I}$ had never held a deformed infant in my arms before. To tell the truth, I had never even seen a deformed infant before. Now here I was responsible for delivering three tiny female orphans to their adoptive parents on Christmas Eve.

Twenty-eight years old, a New England Yankee through and through, I taught English on Cheju Island, Republic of Korea. College students the country-over had been rioting and they had succeeded in closing colleges. I was thoroughly fed up with the many delights and surprises of Korea and needed to go home in the worst way.

One of my colleagues had informed me of the "Baby Flights." A program whereby I could travel from Korea to the U.S. and back for a mere twenty-five percent of the normal airfare.

But the hitch was that the traveler had to transport not one, not two, but THREE infants. That translated into at least three flight changes: Tokyo, Anchorage, and New York. In my case, complete with diapers, formula, pacifiers, and much patience. The alternative was to pay the full fare. Not much of a choice for a single guy in Korea trying to make a buck and stay sane.

I found myself boarding a plane with three infants, aged three months, seven months, and a year-and-half. Training had been a haphazard verbal run through at the orphanage agency the day before.

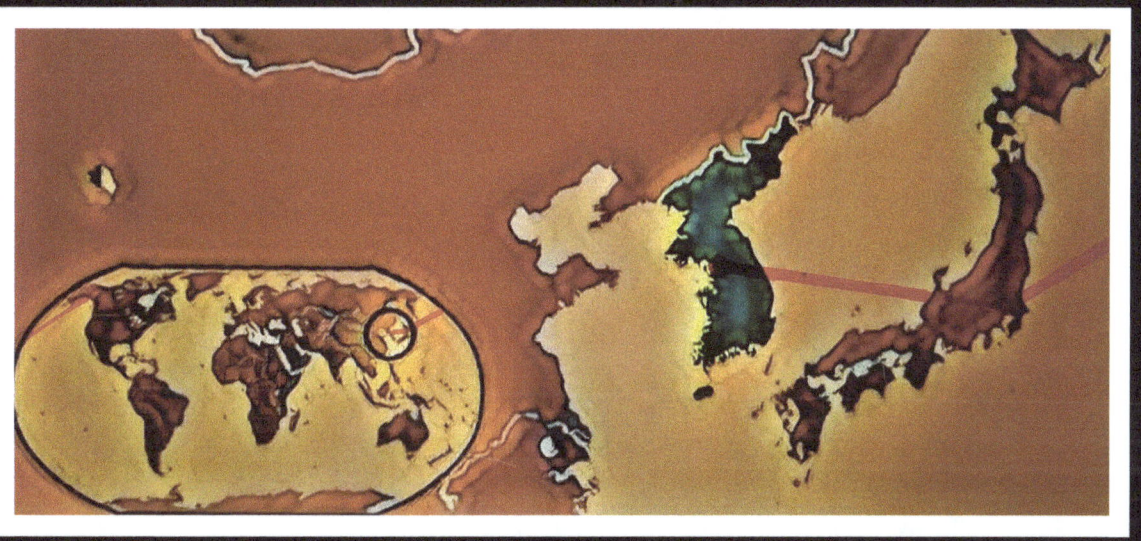

"You will have a double baby carriage." The woman at the agency had told me. She appeared about thirty-five or thirty-six, didn't smile, and couldn't look me in the eyes.

"You will place two babies in the carriage. The third, you will carry in your arms. A document bag will be slung over your right shoulder and a bag of baby necessities will be over your left shoulder."

I cleared my throat for a question, but she belted out more instructions. "You will always be the first one on the plane and the last one off."

I choked on my thoughts and let out a barely audible. "OK."

I had a younger brother and sister. I had changed their diapers. I babysat for them. *What could go wrong? Just how hard could this be?*

When I finally boarded the plane the little ones came complete with runny noses, wet diapers, and colds.

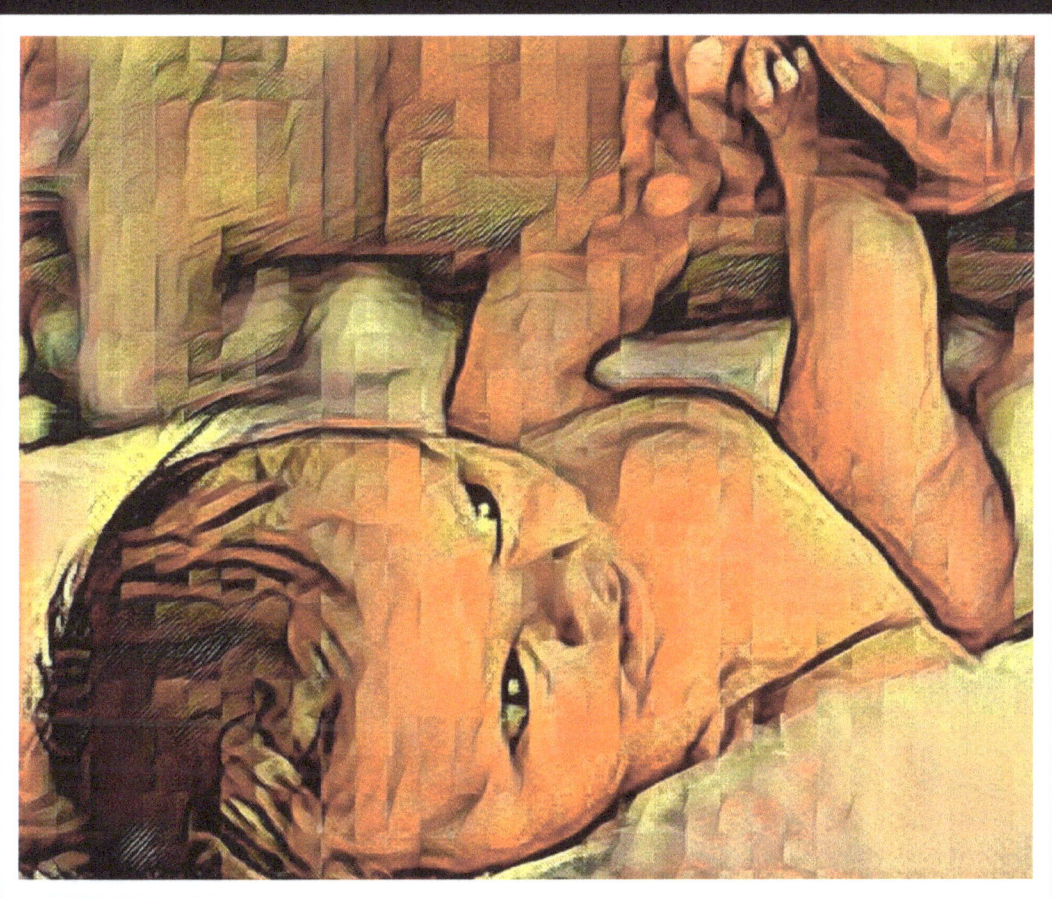

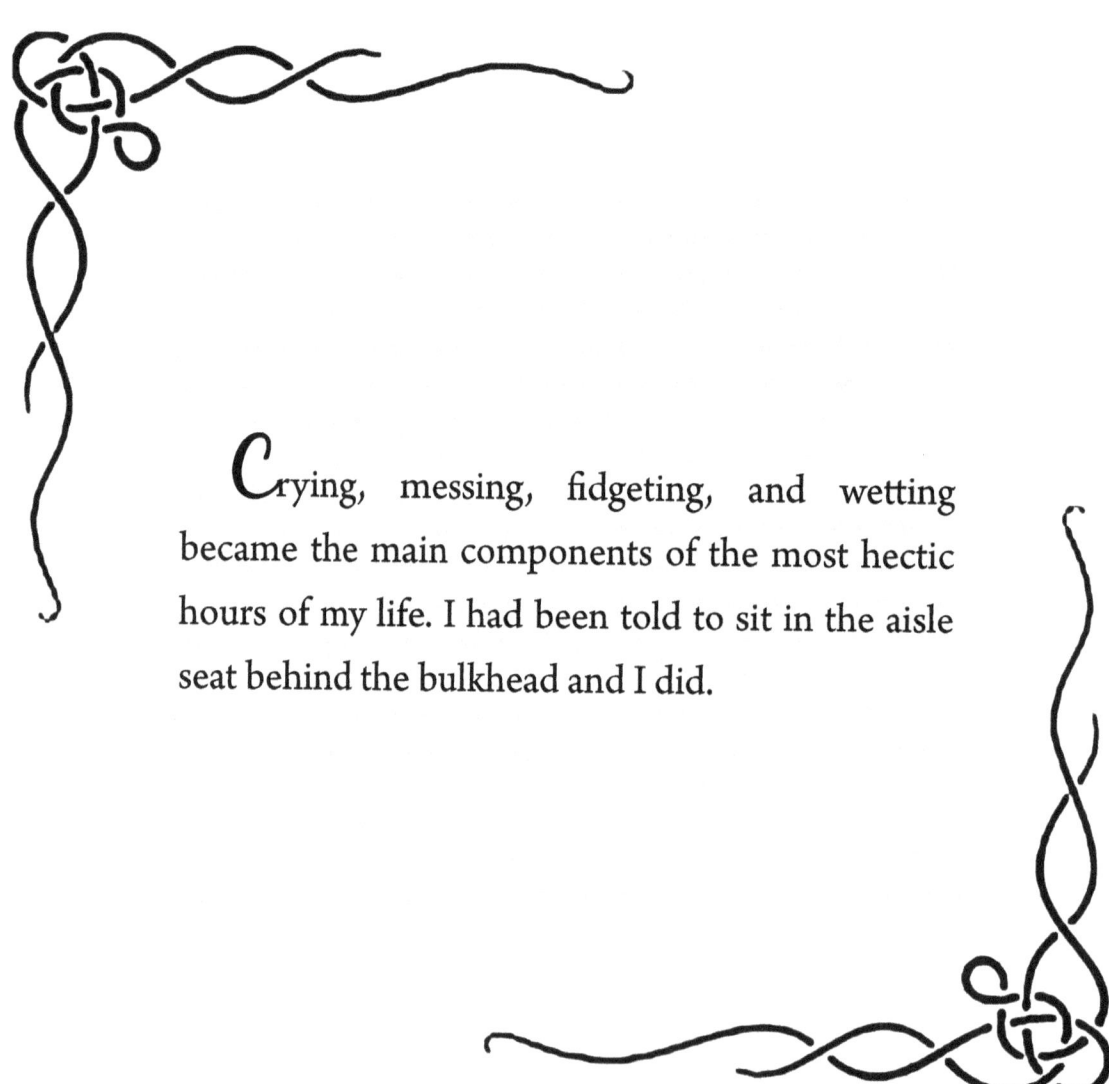

Crying, messing, fidgeting, and wetting became the main components of the most hectic hours of my life. I had been told to sit in the aisle seat behind the bulkhead and I did.

$\mathcal{I}$ placed two babies in their own separate bassinets, which bolted into the wall in front of me and the seat next to me.

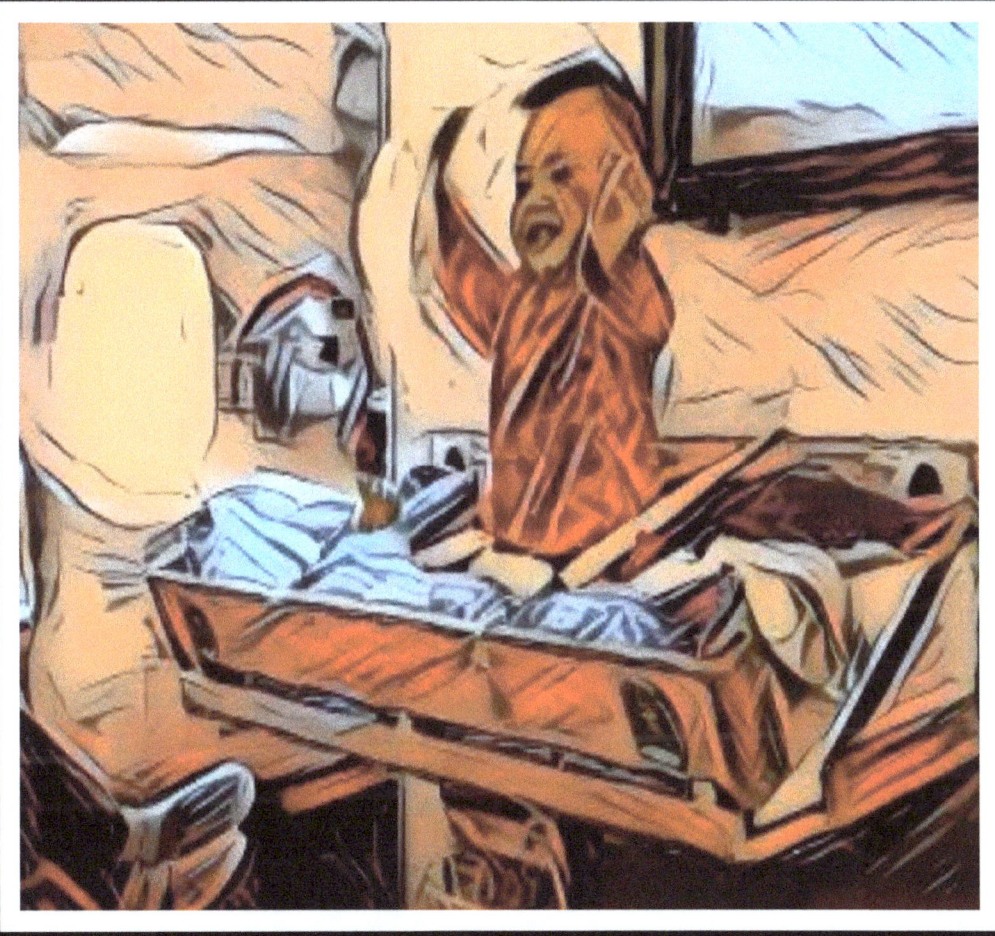

The third baby I had to hold at all times. I stuffed their document bag overhead and their necessity bag under my seat.

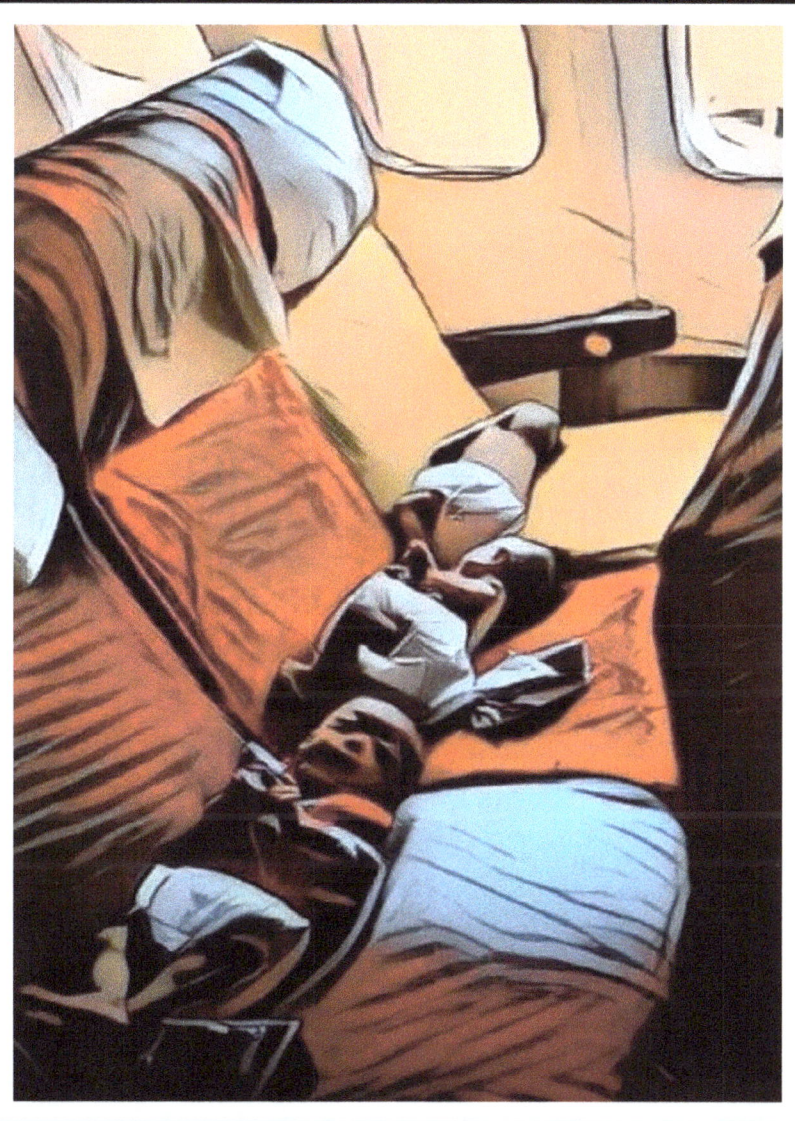

When the plane finally took off, the poor kids let loose with a terrible howl. As the plane climbed, it began to vibrate violently. I'd been on flights many times, nothing approached the jostling we took. Faces grew ashen as the plane continued to shudder, a few passengers whimpered.

Overhead compartments flew open and items rained down on us. I held one baby and leaned forward to protect the one in the nearest bassinet in front of me. The flight attendants hunkered down where they were, grabbing anything to steady themselves.

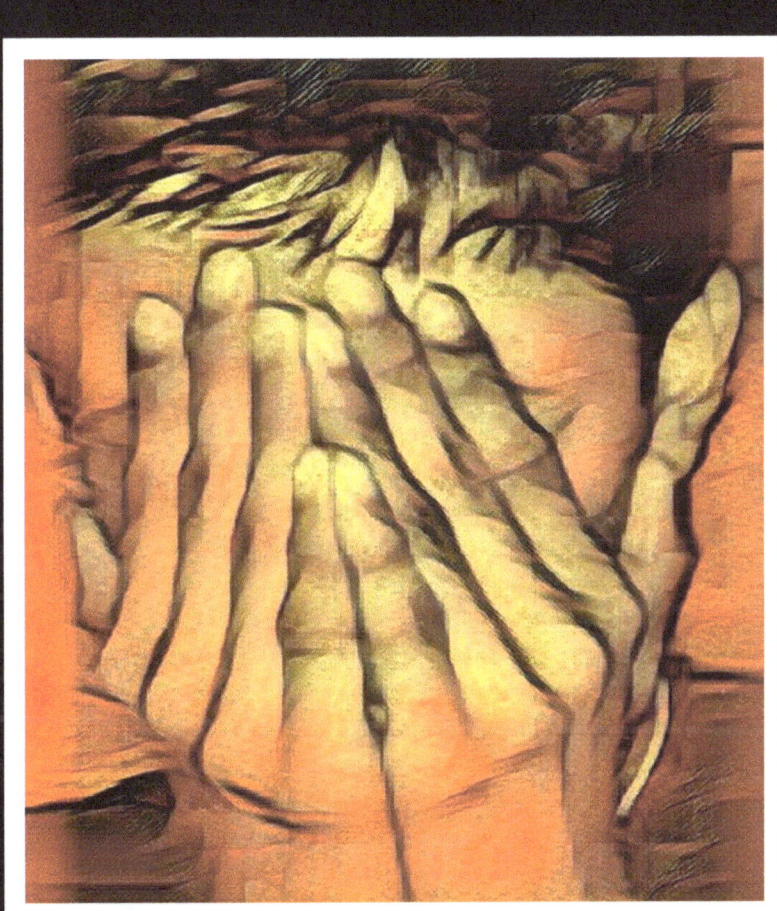

The trembling increased so much all the babies quieted in unison. The plane resounded with noises of shuddering, creaking, but inside the plane people didn't utter a word. *Man, the wings are going to snap. What a way to go.*

A few seconds later, the plane stopped shaking; in unison the babies sucked in air and howled with full lungs.

The entire planeload of passengers burst into tension relieving laughter, and that cut the ice for those kids and me. People slapped each other on the backs.

Some people clapped and the attendants served free drinks for the rest of the flight.

Korea and I hadn't fared so well in the past three months. Exotic and beautiful indeed. But most of the time I didn't think I understood what was going on. Yes didn't mean yes. No did not mean no.

It was a topsy-turvy world for me. It seemed that screwings were a part of the natural order there. For example, the real fat juicy teaching contract I had signed in Connecticut turned out to be somewhat short of the juice and fat once I got there.

But one thing disturbed me a lot and I hadn't had much time to reflect on it. The infant I clutched was deformed to the max and quiet as a mouse. She had a massive head with disproportionately minute arms and fingers. Obviously the poor thing was a dwarf baby. *This child is messed up.* I was surprised with my reaction. I was repulsed AND I began to worry if the new parents on the other side of the Pacific realized what they were having delivered to them.

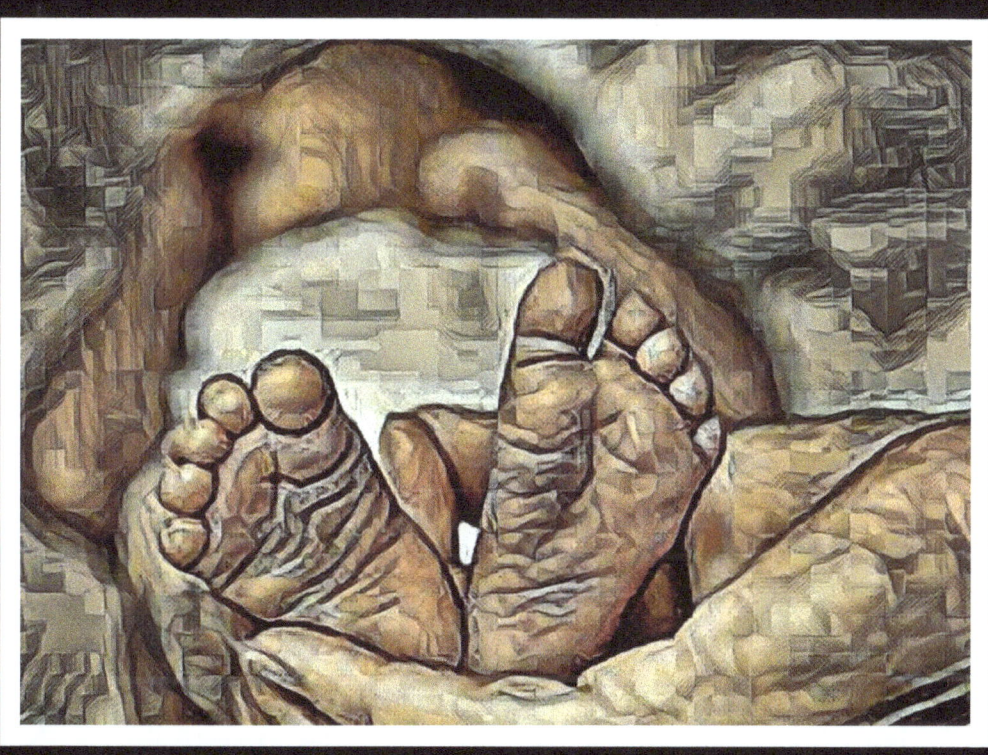

So ... I figured this deformed child was more of Korea pulling a scam on some unsuspecting couple in USA and the nasty part of it—I was the conduit.

Naturally I didn't look forward to the transfer, but I was too busy to give it much consideration. Babies hollered, howled, and screamed. The one on my lap was as wet as an ocean, and the milk formula in the bottles was dropping low. I rapidly remembered how to clean a wet bottom, put on a new diaper, and stick a pacifier in an open mouth.

Two smiling American soldiers, obviously a couple, ambling down the aisle stopped by me.

"They all yours?" asked one of them with a sweet pumpkin-pie-eating southern accent.

"Nope, I'm the deliveryman. You're looking at orphans on their way to a new home."

"Could we … uh … hold em' for a minute or so?"

"Yeah, just make sure you hold their little necks." *Where did that come from?*

So, I sat there alone and watched these two soldiers warm up to these babies like they cradled baskets of thin shelled eggs. The soldiers got smaller as they dawdled down the aisle, and they pulled the babies closer to their faces, whispering to them.

I don't have to worry, they're OK with those two.

I sighed, *Oh God, only one left to watch and she's sleeping.* But when I peered down at the eighteen-month-old baby with the very large head in my lap, I found that not to be true. She stared at me. I noticed her long eyelashes. She's gorgeous! As I looked into her eyes, I couldn't help but see that they held a crisp, intelligent glow. Then she smiled. It surprised me and I was hooked. Funny how things like that can change you. The person on my right in the window seat was out for the count. Nobody was looking so I leaned forward and kissed the child on the forehead. From that point on, she radiated beauty, and she rarely left my arms.

The Tokyo stopover didn't come soon enough for me. The soldiers returned and apologized for not being able to help anymore as they had another flight.

They each handed back a baby. I placed MY baby in the bassinet and proceeded to change the diapers of the two babies the soldiers had just handed me. A pile of single dollar bills fell from the two babies' clothing. *What the heck?* I quickly glanced at the departing soldiers. One of them gave the thumbs-up sign and blurted, "Little varmints' gonna' need all the help they can get; Merry Christmas."

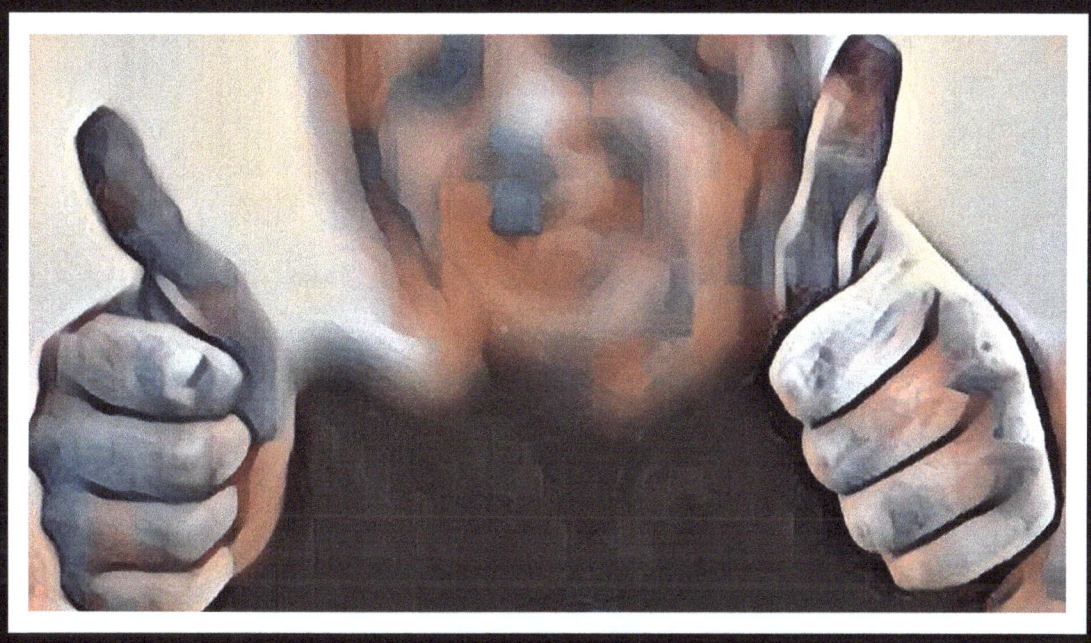

"Thanks," I yelled.

I placed two babies in the double baby carriage, made sure I had a firm grip on mine, and rolled us off the plane to a waiting room. I went to a row of chairs and plunked down still clinging on to my baby. Not many minutes later an attractive Asian woman approached. She hovered nearby, walked up to me and then left. I saw her do an about-face ten feet away and then she plowed straight back.

"Are those babies orphans?" she whispered as she stared down at them.

"Yes, they are."

The woman started crying, "Twenty-four years ago I was one of those kids."

I stood, "Would you like to hold one?"

"I saw you on the flight, but I was afraid to say anything. Could I hold one?"

"Sure, pick one." She unbuckled the one that was awake. "Why don't we put two rows of seats together for a larger area for them?" she suggested.

"Great idea."

We slid two rows of three seats together so the high backs faced outward and the low seat parts merged together like a playpen. The woman sat at one end of our playpen and I at the other.

She held a baby up high with her two hands and I recognized joy and sadness. She then clutched the baby close to her and closed her eyes. I also closed my eyes because for at least a short time the babies didn't cry. A boarding call let me know when it was time to reboard the plane.

"If you help me bring a baby on, you can pre-board the plane with me," I said.

"I'm not ready to give this baby back yet. I would love to continue holding her."

We moved the seats to their original orientation and prepared the kids. I piggy-backed one. The woman, whose name I still did not know, followed me on board with the other two. I headed toward my bulkhead area, placed a sleeping baby in the bassinette, and continued holding mine.

"Can I take this angel to my seat?"

"Absolutely."

The plane filled and some passengers smiled at me, others grimaced. Eventually the plane took off. Once in the air my orphan assistant would show up and lend a hand, clean a bottom, or soothe an unsettled little one.

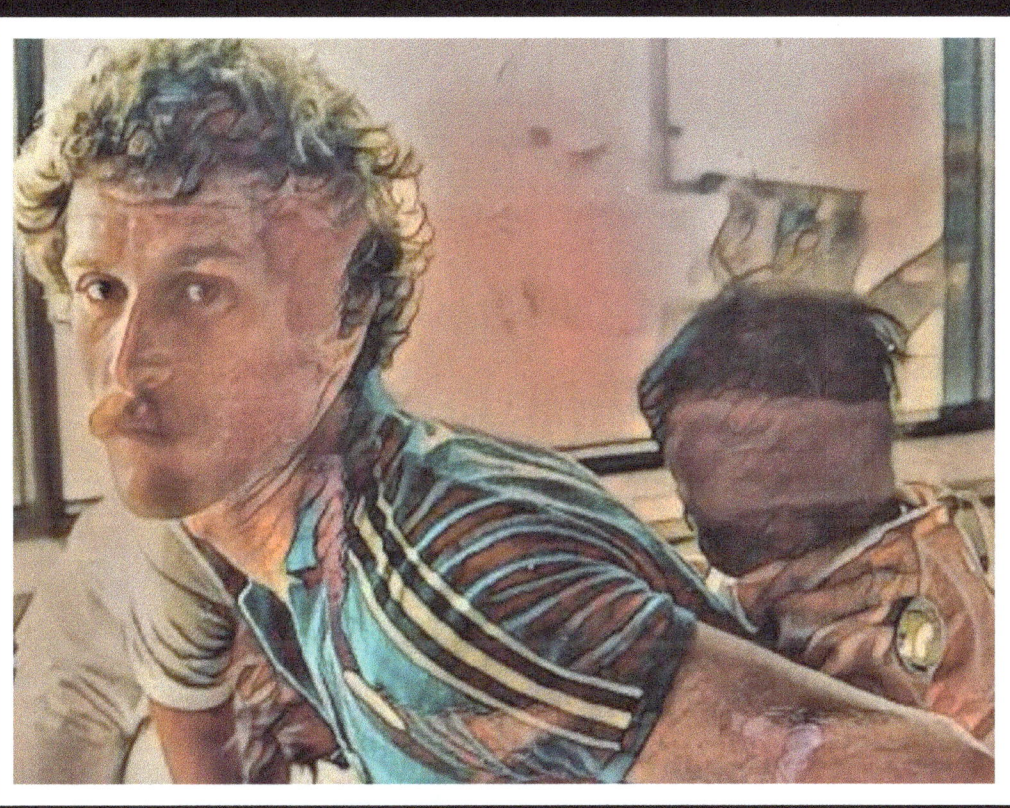

By now I had developed a strong bond with "my" baby. I even named her Tina. The more I thought about giving her to someone else, the more I worried about her prospective parents. I feel like a slave trader and a traitor all wrapped into one.

Seconds slowly dragged out to minutes and then minutes crept to hours. Sleep, magnificent gentle eye-closing sleep ever so sought, remained unavailable.

There never seemed to be a time when all three of the babies slept. And I noticed if a baby anywhere on the plane cried I bolted upright.

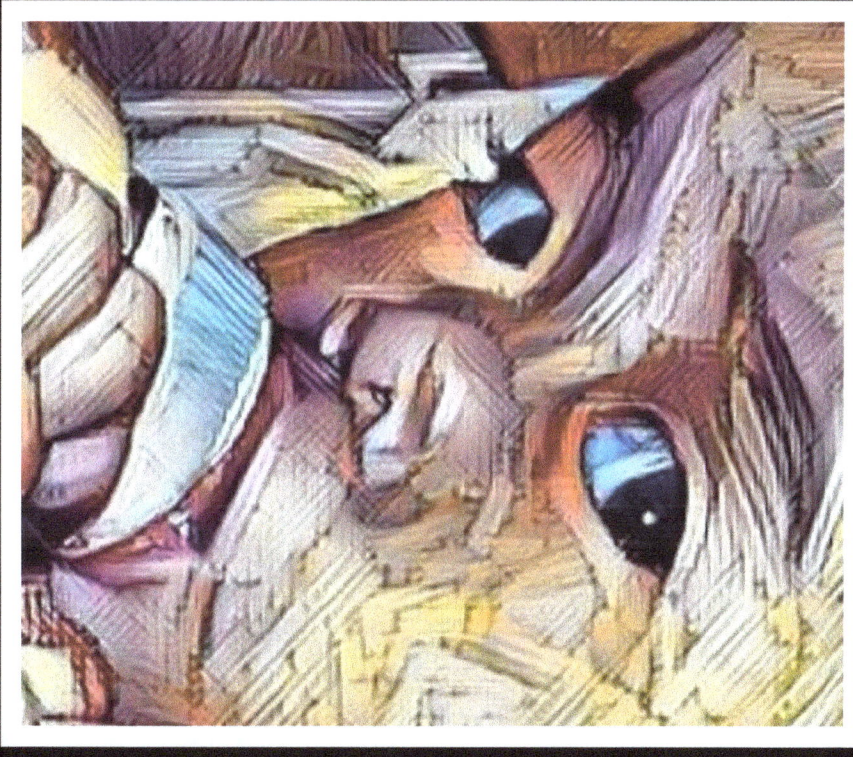

The Anchorage changeover swept past me like an unsubtitled foreign film. I observed things but wasn't really sure what had happened. My hands and body moved, but exhaustion nipped around my edges. I also lost my adoptee helper there. I could hardly remember her handing a baby to me. I was pretty sure I thanked her. My mantra became - *New York, New York, just get me to New York.*

Tired, beat, and sticky under the arm pits, at long last I heard the magic words – "Please place the table in front of you back in its locking position and return your seat to their forward position. We will be landing in New York in ten minutes."

The rough landing bounced us around and the babies who had at long last closed their eyes now opened their mouths. The plane touched the landing strip and I let out a sigh. *First on, last off. Like it or not you have to wait. Well, Tina we'll see what fate has in store for you.*

Passengers collected their things and scrambled off the plane. I had the whole plane to myself, two couples rushed in, matched identification tags and off they sped with their new children. But I still held Tina, and it seemed like nobody was coming on board for her. In the end, I trudged off the plane to a small crowd. Tina cried and clung to me tightly.

What if nobody comes for her?

$\mathcal{I}$ spotted them standing to the side of the exit. ***Perfect! Unbelievable!*** I had to work hard not to stare. The man was no more than four feet tall, and his wife even tinier. They walked toward me and small hands of the dwarf couple reached up for Tina. As I passed Tina, she said, "Oma" to me. Which of course could only mean one thing - Mom. At that point I lost it. I wiped tears from my face, walked to the side of the terminal, crumpled on the carpeted floor, sniffled and wept like a three-year-old.

The following year after another full dose of Korea I paid the full fare home. The Baby Flight was too expensive.

AUTHOR'S NOTE: Over 400,000 copies of *The Baby Flight* story have been published. It won: The Pebbly Beach CA Short Story Contest and The Monterey County Short Story Contest. It was also published in *Open Your Heart, Open Your Soul* (Elodia Tate and Yolanda King). This is the first time it has been illustrated. Paul Karrer and his wife Mi-Ra delivered twelve orphans while they taught in Korea. It was their last baby flight. *The Baby Flight* is entirely non-fiction.

www.ingramcontent.com/pod-product-compliance
Lightning Source LLC
Chambersburg PA
CBHW051248110526
44588CB00025B/2922